Super-Flea
and Other
Animal Champions

Chicago, Illinois

A division of Reed Elsevier, Inc.
Chicago, Illinois

Customer Service 888–363–4266

Visit our website at www.heinemannraintree.com

Printed and bound in the United States by Lake Book Manufacturing, Inc.

10 09 08 07 06
10 9 8 7 6 5 4 3 2 1

Library of Congress Cataloging-in-Publication Data
Spilsbury, Louise.
    Super-flea and other animal champions : cells, tissues, and organs / Louise and Richard Spilsbury.
        p. cm.
    Includes bibliographical references and index.
    ISBN 1-4109-1937-4 (library binding) -- ISBN 1-4109-1968-4 (pbk.)
    1. Animal locomotion--Juvenile literature. 2. Animal physiology--Juvenile literature. 3. Reading--Remedial teaching--Juvenile literature. I. Spilsbury, Richard, 1963- II. Title.
    QP301.S757 2005
    591.5'7--dc22

                        2005009547

Acknowledgments
The author and publishers are grateful to the following for permission to reproduce copyright material: Getty Images/Allsport p. 16 (top); Getty Images/The Image Bank pp. 10–11, 27; Getty/Photodisc pp. 4–5, 28 (top), 28 (bottom); Getty Images/Photographer's Choice pp. 6–7, 27; Nature Picture Library pp. 24–25, 27 (Michael Richards/John Downer); NHPA pp. 18–19, 27 (Stephen Dalton), 29 (David and Irene Myers); oceanwideimages.com pp. 14–15 (C. and M. Fallows); Photolibrary.com/Dynamic Graphics (UK) Ltd. pp. 20–21, 22–23, 27; Photolibrary.com pp. 12–13, 27 (Thomas Haider); Science Photo Library/Eye of Science pp. 16 (bottom), 17; Science Photo Library pp. 8–9 (Andrew Syred).

Cover photograph of a human flea, reproduced with permission of Photolibrary.com/Okapia.

Illustrations by Seb Burnett.

The publishers would like to thank Nancy Harris and Harold Pratt for their assistance in the preparation of this book.

Every effort has been made to contact copyright holders of any material reproduced in this book. Any omissions will be rectified in subsequent printings if notice is given to the publishers.

The paper used to print this book comes from sustainable resources.

Disclaimer
All the Internet addresses (URLs) given in this book were valid at the time of going to press. However, due to the dynamic nature of the Internet, some addresses may have changed, or sites may have changed or ceased to exist since publication. While the author and publishers regret any inconvenience this may cause readers, no responsibility for any such changes can be accepted by either the author or the publishers.

Contents

Some words are printed in bold, **like this**. You can find out what they mean on page 30. You can also look in the box at the bottom of the page where they first appear.

Welcome to the Championships

People compete against each other in athletic championships. But what if there were animal championships? We are going to find out which animals would win the different events. We will look at:

- The deepest divers
- The highest jumpers
- The fastest sprinters
- The strongest lifters, and more!

cell   basic unit that all living things are made from
microscope   special instrument that makes very tiny objects look big enough for us to see

The animals we will meet are not champions because they train in a gym. The reason for their success is the **cells** in their bodies. Cells are the basic units that make up all living things. Most animals are made up of millions of different kinds of cells. The different cells form different parts of an animal's body.

◄*These fireworks are to celebrate the start of the Animal Championships!*

Cell-spotting

*Your body is made of millions of cells. Cells are so tiny you can only see them with a special instrument called a **microscope**. A microscope makes things look bigger than they really are.*

World-Class Climber

First, we are going to check out the climbing competition. The tokay gecko would be the clear winner. This lizard is a world-class climber. It can climb up a smooth wall in seconds. How does the gecko do it?

It looks like the gecko has glue on its feet. Yet the gecko does not cheat. This champion grips the wall using only the hair under its toes.

A sticky business

Geckos can climb smooth and slippery surfaces quickly. They can hang from a ceiling using just one hairy toe!

◄The tokay gecko is a lizard. It uses its climbing skills to chase flies to eat.

Meet the athlete: the gecko

So, why are geckos the champion climbers? The parts of an animal's body are made up of different kinds of **cells**. Special cells make up the hairs on a gecko's toes. These hairs help it to climb.

Each toe on a gecko's foot is covered with clumps of tiny hairs. The cells at the tip of each hair are shaped like small suckers. A gecko can stick to almost any surface. This is because of the sucker cells on its toes.

Suckers!

Some scientists are trying to make a material that will be like a gecko's toes. One day, people may be able to walk up walls wearing socks made from this material!

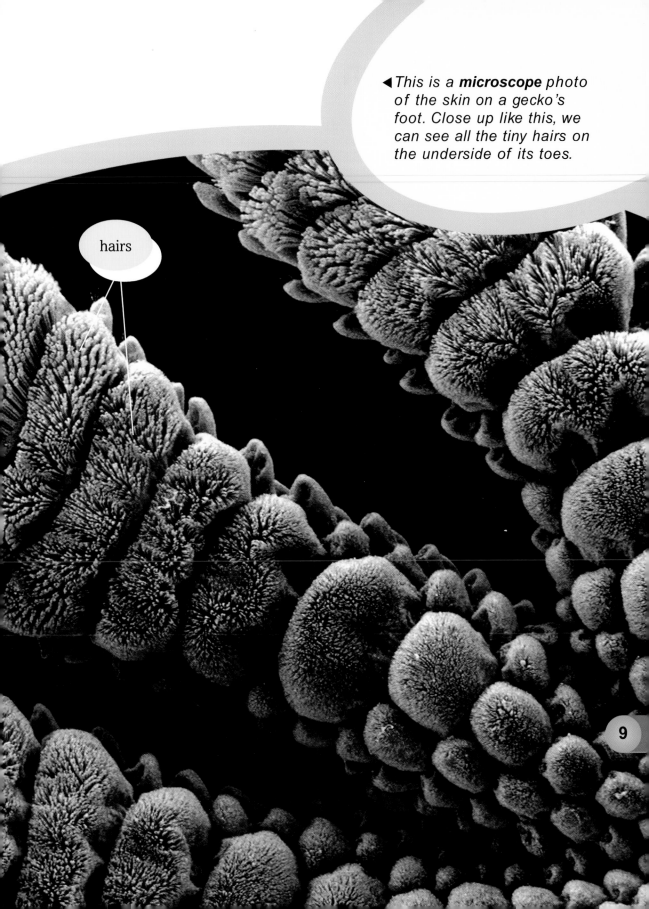

hairs

◀ *This is a **microscope** photo of the skin on a gecko's foot. Close up like this, we can see all the tiny hairs on the underside of its toes.*

9

Super-Flea High Jumper

The flea is the favorite to win the high jump event. Wow, what a jump! It is over in an instant.

The flea uses the **tissues** in its legs to jump so high. Tissues are groups of **cells** that work together to do a particular job. First, the flea bends its back legs. This squeezes together a pad of rubbery tissue in its knees.

Then, *boing*! The pad of rubbery tissue expands. The flea's legs straighten. This movement makes the flea spring high into the air.

The really high jump!

A flea can jump 130 times the height of its own body. That is like a person jumping over the Eiffel Tower in Paris, France!

tissue   group of similar cells that work together to do a particular job

▲ When the flea's back legs straighten, they push the flea up into the air at high speed.

Deepest Diver

The sperm whale would be the winner of the diving event. It would also be the biggest animal in the championships.

The sperm whale is about 46 feet (14 meters) long. It dives underwater by flicking its powerful, 13-foot- (4-meter-) wide tail. Only 20 minutes later, the whale reaches a depth of 1.5 miles (2.5 kilometers). That's about the length of 30 football fields!

The sperm whale needs to breathe air. Yet it can stay underwater for a long time. The whale does this by taking huge gulps of air before it dives.

The sperm whale stores **oxygen** from this air in its **muscles**. Each muscle is made up of millions of muscle **cells**. The oxygen stored in the muscle cells keeps the sperm whale going.

◀ *A sperm whale can hold its breath for about one hour underwater. Then, it needs to come to the surface to breathe again.*

muscle body part that helps living things move
oxygen gas in air that living things need

Speed–Swimming Sensation

In short-distance swimming events, the mako shark is a sensation. It can race through the water at 68 miles (110 kilometers) per hour.

The mako shark is the world's fastest shark. The shark swims by moving its large tail from side to side. The shape of its body helps it to cut swiftly through the water. The shark's **fins** help to keep it balanced. The fins also help the shark to steer at high speed.

fin flap or fold of skin that helps a fish to swim

▼ For short distances, the mako shark can race at a high speed through the water.

fin

Fast food!

The mako shark's high speed is very useful. It means the shark can catch fast-swimming fish, such as tuna. Most other sharks are too slow to catch these fish.

Meet the athlete: the shark

Why is the mako shark a champion swimmer? One secret of the shark's success is its skin!

A mako shark's skin is covered in lots of **scales**. These scales are shaped like sharp teeth. Scales are pieces of hard skin. They overlap, like the tiles on a roof. The shape of the scales lets water flow quickly past them. This means water does not slow the shark down as it swims.

The scales are a type of **tissue**. They are made up of special skin **cells**. Among the cells there are also small chunks of crystal. These chunks of crystal are very hard. They help to make the scales tough and keep their shape.

▲Some swimmers wear full-body swimsuits, like this.

◀The swimsuits have a surface like a shark's skin. This helps swimmers race faster through the water.

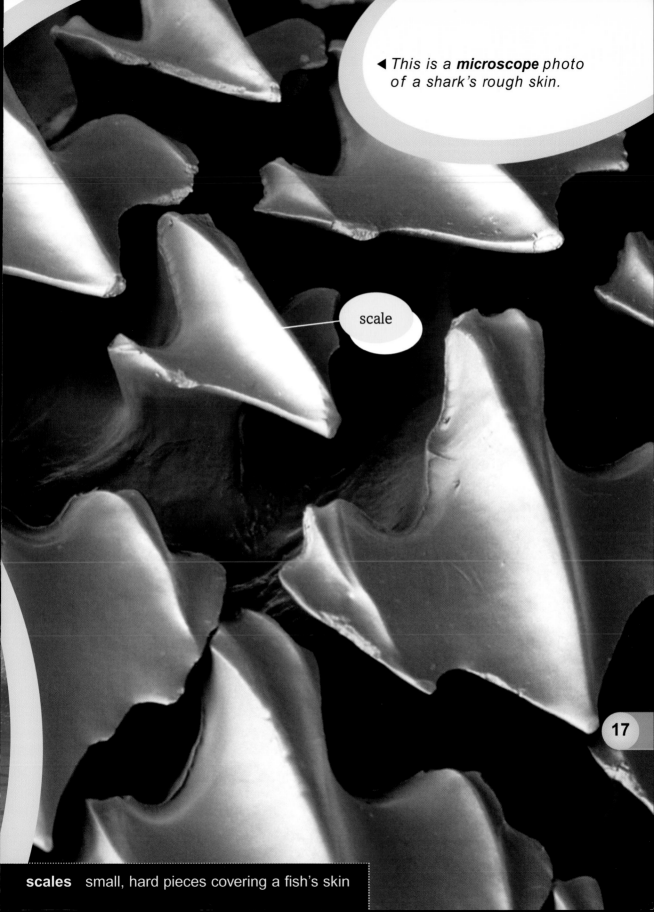

◀ *This is a **microscope** photo of a shark's rough skin.*

scale

scales   small, hard pieces covering a fish's skin

Winning Weight Lifter

For its size, the rhinoceros beetle is the strongest animal on Earth. It can lift 850 times its own weight! An elephant can lift only a quarter of its own weight.

You have to admire this insect's body. It has a tough, shiny covering. This covering is made of strong skin **tissue**. The tissue is about 0.04 inches (1 millimeter) thick over most of the beetle's body. However, the horns are made of thicker tissue. This makes them even stronger.

Big head?

A rhinoceros beetle gets its name from the horns on its head. They look like the horns of a rhinoceros. The beetles often use these horns to wrestle with other beetles!

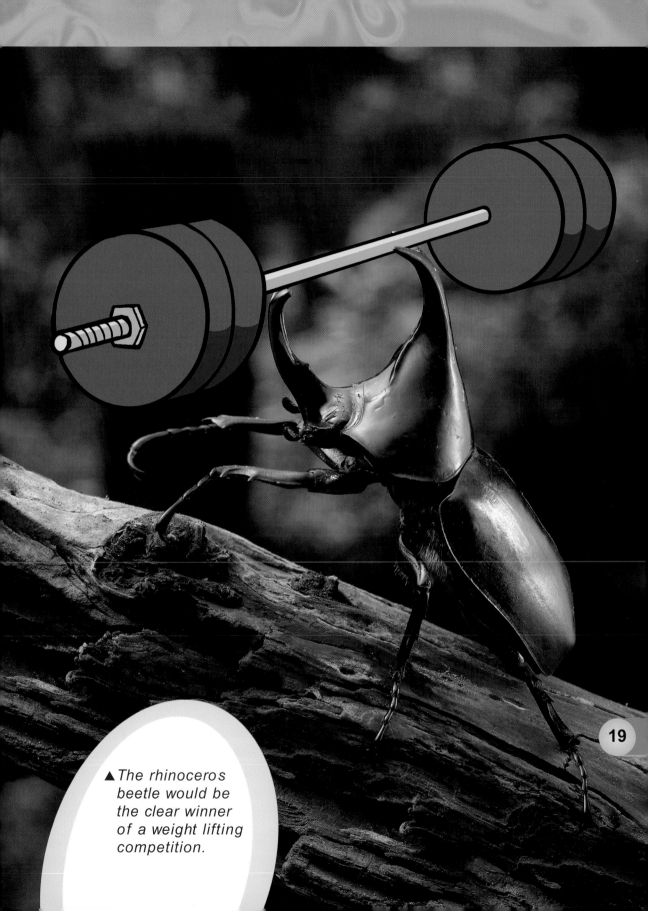

▲The rhinoceros beetle would be the clear winner of a weight lifting competition.

Supreme Sprinter

Just look at this champion run! The cheetah can go from 0 to 60 miles (0 to 100 kilometers) per hour as quickly as a sports car.

The secret of the cheetah's speedy success is in its backbone, or **spine**. The cheetah's backbone is **flexible**. This means it can bend easily.

The cheetah's spine arches up high when its front feet touch the ground. This allows the back legs to reach forward and land ahead of the front legs! Then, the cheetah pushes off from its back legs. It speeds away again.

Born to run

The cheetah is the fastest animal on land. It can run over 100 yards in 3 seconds. That is three times quicker than the fastest human sprinter!

flexible bends easily in different directions
spine backbone

▼Cheetahs take huge strides with their long legs. When they are running at full speed, it can look as if they are flying through the air!

Meet the athlete: the cheetah

An animal's **spine** is an **organ**. An organ is a body part made of different kinds of **tissue**. The cheetah's spine is strong and **flexible** because it contains two kinds of tissue. It has bone tissue and **ligament** tissue.

Bone is a tissue made of bone **cells**. The bones in a cheetah's spine are strong and hard. They are joined to each other with strips of bendy ligament.

Ligament tissue is made up of rubbery ligament cells. The ligaments allow the bones of the spine to stretch out and bend up.

A heavy tail helps a cheetah keep its balance when it changes direction at high speed.

ligament   rubbery tissue that holds bones in joints together
organ   body part made of different kinds of tissue

A flexible spine and long legs help the cheetah take long strides as it runs.

Cheetahs have sharp claws. These grip the ground like the spikes on a sprinter's shoes.

23

Sharp-Shooting Spitter

The spitting cobra is not the most popular animal! Yet in a sharp-shooting contest, everyone would be impressed with the cobra's aim.

The spitting cobra shoots **venom** instead of arrows. Venom is a kind of liquid poison. The snake makes the venom in a special **organ** inside its head. This organ is made from different types of **tissue**.

The organ is a like a small balloon. **Muscles** in the snake's head can squeeze the balloon. This makes venom shoot out through narrow tubes in the cobra's fangs.

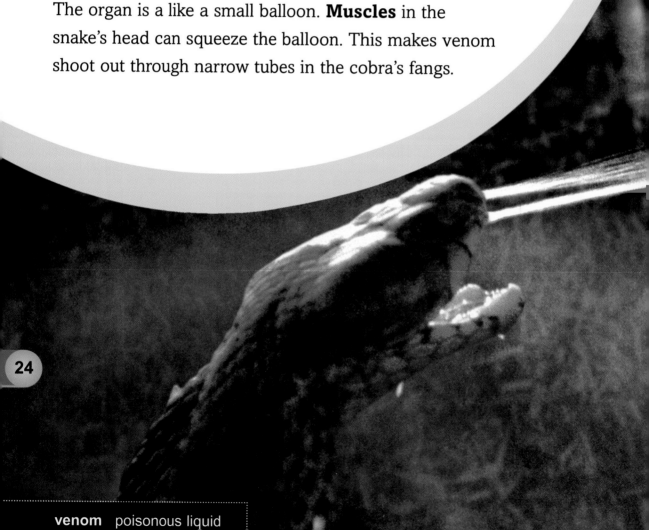

venom poisonous liquid

▼ The sharp-shooting cobra can spray its venom a distance of 8 feet (2.5 meters) away.

Spit attack

Spitting cobras usually spray venom at animals that might attack them. The venom causes terrible pain. It can even make another animal blind.

Secrets of Their Success

All these animals are champions because of their **cells**. Cells are the building blocks of all body parts. Groups of similar cells form **tissues**. **Organs** are made from more than one type of tissue. The cheetah's **spine** is an organ. It is made of more than one type of tissue.

When human athletes win sporting events, their prizes are medals, money, and fame. Yet the animals in this book are not given prizes. Animals use their skills and body parts to escape from danger, or to catch a meal! An animal's reward is survival.

Skill	Reason	Animal
Speed	To catch fast-moving food	Mako shark, cheetah
Deep diving	To find food deep in the oceans	Sperm whale
Jumping	To land on an animal to feed	Flea
Climbing	To find food and escape danger	Tokay gecko
Weight lifting	To push aside other beetles	Rhinoceros beetle
Sharp shooting	To scare off attackers	Spitting cobra

Cheetah

SPEED 1st

Flea

Sperm whale

DEEP DIVING 1st

Tokay gecko

JUMPING 1st

Rhinoceros beetle

Spitting cobra

CLIMBING 1st

SHARP SHOOTING 1st

WEIGHT LIFTING 1st

▼*These animals are champions because they were born with the right stuff!*

27

More Animal Record-Breakers

Check out these amazing animal record-breakers.

The longest **cell** is found in the giraffe. A nerve cell goes from its head all the way to its toes. It can be 16 feet (5 meters) long.

Skin is a type of **tissue**. The chameleon can change the color of its skin. A chameleon's skin contains cells that are full of ink. The cells can squeeze together or spread out to change the color of the skin.

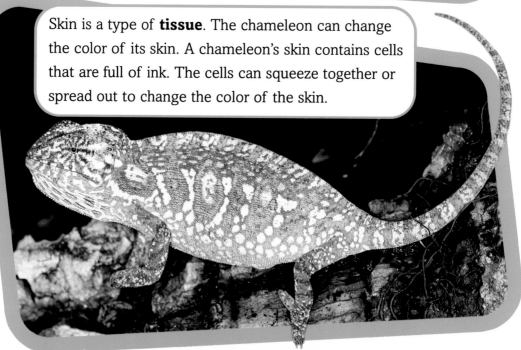

Remember . . .

- **Cells** are the basic units that all living things are made of. Some living things are made from just one cell. Others are made from billions of cells.

- **Tissues** are groups of similar cells. Common types of animal tissues are **muscle** and blood tissue.

- **Organs** are groups of different tissues that join together to do a particular job.

A heart is an **organ**. Its job is to pump blood around the body. A blue whale has enough blood to fill a swimming pool. It needs a heart the size of a small car to pump the blood around its body.

Glossary

cell basic unit that all living things are made of. There are many different kinds of cells, including muscle, skin, and bone cells.

fin flap or fold of skin that helps a fish to swim. Fish may have fins on their back, belly, and sides.

flexible bends easily in different directions. A cheetah's spine is flexible.

ligament rubbery tissue that holds bones in joints together. A cheetah's spine is made up of stretchy ligament tissue and hard bone tissue.

microscope special instrument that makes very tiny objects look big enough for us to see. You can only see most cells through a powerful microscope.

muscle body part that helps living things move. For example, leg muscles make leg bones move.

organ body part made of different kinds of tissue. A spine is an organ made up of bone tissue and ligament tissue.

oxygen gas in air that living things need

scales small, hard pieces covering a fish's skin. Different kinds of fish have scales in different shapes and sizes.

spine backbone. A cheetah's spine is strong and flexible.

tissue group of similar cells that work together to do a particular job. For example, muscle cells form muscle tissue to move legs.

venom poisonous liquid. Cobras spit venom through fangs in their mouth.

Want to Know More?

Books

- Butterfield, Moira. *Genetics*. Mankato, Minn.: Smart Apple Media, 2003.

- Snedden, Robert. *Cell Division & Genetics*. Chicago: Heinemann Library, 2003.

- Wallace, Holly. *Cells and Systems*. Chicago: Heinemann Library, 2001.

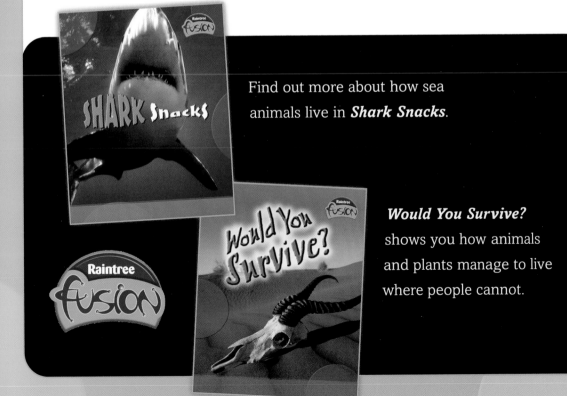

Find out more about how sea animals live in **Shark Snacks**.

Would You Survive? shows you how animals and plants manage to live where people cannot.

Index